Peacemakers

PEOPLE YOU NEED TO KNOW

SUSANNA WRIGHT

WAYLAND

First published in Great Britain in 2022
by Wayland
Copyright © Hodder and Stoughton, 2022
Illustrations copyright © 2022
by Susanna Wright

Wayland, an imprint of
Hachette Children's Group
Part of Hodder and Stoughton
Carmelite House
50 Victoria Embankment
London EC4Y 0DZ

An Hachette UK Company
www.hachette.co.uk
www.hachettechildrens.co.uk

HB ISBN 978 1 5263 0596 1
PB ISBN 978 1 5263 0597 8

MIX
Paper from
responsible sources
FSC® C104740
FSC
www.fsc.org

Printed and bound in Dubai

Design by Cathryn Gilbert and Peter Scoulding
Edited by Paul Rockett

Contents

Peacemakers

Woven into human behaviour since the evolution of the species, the hardwired capacity for conflict has shaped history. The earliest evidence of violence between humans ever discovered – fossilised remains of victims of the Nataruk massacre found in a lagoon in eastern Africa – is estimated as dating from ten thousand years ago. As humanity and societies evolved, the desire to find resolution – to create peace in the face of war – developed alongside it. Through the centuries, rare and important individuals have stepped forward in order to counteract the primitive push towards war: the peacemakers.

Sometimes the quest for peace is a fight in itself. There are those who knew that in striving to save the lives of countless others, they might lose their own life. And there are those who reached out to their enemies to try to find common ground.

A peacemaker may be an individual or part of an organisation who is moved to negotiate with warring groups and arbitrate between them in an attempt to mediate and move them into non-violent dialogue. A peacemaker can also be someone who works for the liberation of those who are oppressed, or a person who writes or speaks fluently about the need for peace, inspiring change.

There are many peace organisations in existence today – international, national and local – which promote peace and non-violent alternatives to conflict, seeking to find powerful ways to alleviate the brutality of war. Their aim is always to restore harmony and therefore reduce human suffering.

The people included in this book are a few notable examples of what it means to be a peacemaker and each has their own unique story of applied courage and compassion; each has impacted the world for the better. Ultimately the objective for peacemakers always comes back to the same thing: the belief that every human being deserves respect, freedom and to live in safety. The centring of that belief is as vital today as it ever has been.

LAOZI

> *If you are at peace you are living in the present.*

LAOZI – which means 'Old Master' – was an ancient Chinese philosopher, poet and writer. He is said to be the author of the *Tao Te Ching*, a classic Chinese text that is fundamental to Taoism. Taoism is a philosophical tradition that emphasises living in harmony with nature, being in the moment and embracing 'the way'. 'Tao' can be translated as 'road' or 'way', and so Taoism is a pathway – via meditation, mindfulness and visualisation – to a sense of the limitless Universe and of being in the moment: to go with the flow, live a simple life and accept yourself. In Taoist terms, this is the way to inner peace.

Laozi, a scholar who worked as the Keeper of Archives in the royal court in China in the sixth century BCE, was never a formal teacher. However, he attracted a great many loyal students who came to hear him speak about the four cardinal virtues: respect for all life, sincerity, gentleness and supportiveness. He believed that if we love and honour ourselves, this love will then flow outwards towards all beings and that if that love is expressed as respect, gratitude and kindness, then we can all live in peace and harmony. His vision was to create a peaceful world, one individual at a time.

Modern scientific research has confirmed that the practical application of Laozi's teachings – mindfulness, meditation and gratitude – is proven to increase human happiness and wellness. One of the great world religions, Taoism continues to be practised by people in China and throughout the world.

NANYE'HI / NANCY WARD

c. 1738 – 1822

" Our cry is all for peace, let it continue.
This peace must last forever. "

Born in a time of great conflict in America, NANYE'HI – later NANCY WARD – was a Cherokee woman who made it her responsibility to try to establish peace among warring factors: American troops, European settlers and the Cherokee Nation who had lived in the region for thousands of years.

As a child, Ward was known as Wild Rose, and then as Nanye'hi: 'one who is with the Spirit People', after having a vision of spirits guiding her home. She later married a Cherokee warrior called Kingfisher; when he was killed in an intertribal battle in 1775 she took up her husband's rifle and led the Cherokees to victory. To honour her bravery, the Cherokee Nation named her Beloved Woman. As part of the tribal council of chiefs she had the power to save the lives of prisoners, and many white settlers were spared thanks to her compassion.

All too aware of the losses of war, Ward came to believe in peaceful coexistence – to trade with and befriend the settlers. She married an English trader, adopted their farming methods and became the first Cherokee cattle owner and dairy farmer. In 1781 she helped negotiate a peace treaty between the Cherokees and the Americans. She gave a moving speech, after which it was agreed that the Cherokees could retain some of their land. In her old age Ward became a legendary figure; she took in orphans and, after a vision (which later proved accurate) of the Cherokees being displaced and forced to walk countless miles, she urged her tribe not to sell any more of their land.

ERUERA MAIHI PATUONE

c.1764 – 19 SEPTEMBER 1872

Ko te whaiti a Ripia!
(We are small in number but valiant in battle!)

A warrior who came to embody the quest for peace, ERUERA MAIHI PATUONE was a Māori rangatira (chief) of the Ngāti Hao of Hokianga, on the North Island of New Zealand. Patuone lived an extraordinarily long and influential life, helping to shape key events in New Zealand's history and promote peaceful negotiations. As a child he was one of the first Māori people to have contact with Europeans when James Cook's ship visited in 1769, and throughout his life he grew to be very interested in the potential advantages of European settlement. The arrival of the settlers (known as 'Pākehā' or non-Māori usually of British ethnic origin or background) had long been prophesied in Māori lore, and Patuone viewed it as irreversible; a new era had to be embraced as peacefully as possible.

Known as Peacemaker, Patuone was also called the Father of the Pākehā, since his protection made their assimilation less fraught with dangers. In 1835, Patuone was one of the Māori chiefs to sign He Whakaputanga, the Declaration of Independence of the United Tribes of New Zealand. This bold display of indigenous power declared that authority in the land would be with the Confederation of United Tribes, which was made up of Māori leaders. In return for their protection of British subjects in their territory, they sought the British king's protection from other nations. In 1840, Patuone signed the Treaty of Waitangi, which guaranteed full rights of ownership of Māori lands and ensured that Māoris were given the rights of British citizens.

A major player in a developing nation, Patuone was renowned as a warm, courageous proponent of Māori rights and peace between his people and the European settlers.

HENRY DUNANT

8 MAY, 1828 – 30 OCTOBER, 1910

Our real enemy is not the neighbouring country; it's hunger, poverty, ignorance, superstition and prejudice.

A Swiss humanitarian, HENRY DUNANT's life was one of extremes: born into wealth, he died in a hospice after a long period of abject poverty; having enjoyed business success, he neglected his work in favour of peace activism, and in the middle of this, he campaigned for and founded the Red Cross. In doing so, he saved countless lives.

In 1859, Dunant's business interests took him to Solferino in Italy, where a battle was raging. There he witnessed the horrifying ravages of war: the dead and wounded lay everywhere, with minimal to no medical care. Overwhelmed by the suffering he saw, his experiences led him to write a book, *A Memory of Solferino*, in which he imagined the possibility of a voluntary aid society that could provide help for the wounded during wartime.

Dunant travelled through Europe promoting his vision of a neutral organisation created to alleviate suffering. The increasing popularity of his ideas led to the formation of the International Committee of the Red Cross. As a result of this, a conference was held in 1864, which led to an event of huge historical significance: twelve nations signing a commitment to protect wounded soldiers on the battlefield – The Geneva Convention. In recognition of his vision and achievements, Dunant was awarded the Nobel Peace Prize in 1901 along with fellow peace activist Frédéric Passy.

LEO TOLSTOY

9 SEPTEMBER, 1828 – 20 NOVEMBER, 1910

 *If everyone fought for their own convictions there would be no war.*

A Russian novelist whose two most famous books – *War and Peace* (1869) and *Anna Karenina* (1877) – continue to be considered amongst the most profound ever written, TOLSTOY began his adult life as a privileged aristocrat and ended it as an avowed pacifist. He believed fervently in Christian anarchy, which maintains that the authority of God, as expressed in the teachings of Jesus, is greater than that of human society.

This transformation followed a spiritual awakening after a period of great despair for Tolstoy (potentially caused by his experiences during his years as a soldier in the Crimean War, 1853–1856). He captured this struggle in his short non-fiction work *A Confession* (1882). Tormented by what he had done and seen as a young man, he developed pacifist ideas on non-violent resistance, which influenced many vital twentieth-century thinkers such as Gandhi and Martin Luther King, Jr. Indeed, Tolstoy and Gandhi wrote to each other about the ethics of peace and the human spirit in the last year of Tolstoy's life.

It was deeply influential for a writer of such fame and stature as Tolstoy to communicate so passionately the need for peaceful resistance to violence – a need expressed with great clarity in his work of 1894, *The Kingdom of God Is Within You*. He was nominated for both the Nobel Peace Prize and the Nobel Prize in Literature multiple times, and although he won neither he is still remembered and praised all over the world for his writing and philosophy.

BERTHA VON SUTTNER

9 JUNE, 1843 – 21 JUNE, 1914

> "One of the eternal truths is that happiness is created and developed in peace."

BERTHA VON SUTTNER was the pacifist mastermind who influenced the creation of the Nobel Peace Prize. Born in Prague when it was part of the Austrian Empire, Von Suttner grew up in a family on the fringes of aristocracy. In 1873, she travelled to Vienna to be a teacher-companion. Here she met the man she would marry. However prior to the marriage the disapproval of his family prompted her to flee to Paris to take up a position as the secretary to Alfred Nobel, the renowned inventor and engineer. She only stayed for one week, but it was impactful enough to spark a life-long friendship.

After she was married, Von Suttner made a living through teaching but she devoted increasing energy to writing, developing the concept that only through the pursuit of peace could humanity achieve real progress. To aid the cause of pro-peace organisations, Von Suttner wrote her most famous work: *Die Waffen nieder! (Lay Down Your Arms)*, published in 1889. An immediate success, it was a strong condemnation of the horrors of war.

Von Suttner became a prominent leader in the peace movement, establishing peace groups and attending meetings internationally. She sought to convince her friend Nobel of the necessity of the peace movement. A very wealthy man, he responded: "Inform me, convince me, and then I will do something great for the movement", suggesting that he was considering establishing a peace prize. After his death three years later in 1896, people learned that he had set aside a large sum of money for creating the Nobel Prizes. In 1905 Von Suttner herself became the first woman to be awarded the Nobel Peace Prize for her tireless commitment to pacifism.

MOHANDAS KARAMCHAND GANDHI

2 OCTOBER, 1869 – 30 JANUARY, 1948

 In a gentle way, you can shake the world.

MOHANDAS KARAMCHAND GANDHI, a revered anti-colonialist known as 'Mahatma' – meaning 'great soul' – embodied the power of non-violent resistance to injustice. He led a successful campaign to free India from British rule, inspiring civil rights movements all over the world.

Born into a Hindu family in the state of Gujarat in western India, Gandhi trained as a lawyer and moved to South Africa. The Indian community there was subject to discrimination, against which Gandhi was moved to protest with civil disobedience (the peaceful refusal to obey unjust laws). On his return to India in 1915, Gandhi encouraged Indian workers to protest against the crippling land-tax demanded by the British Raj (the British Empire ruling in India). He became leader of the Indian National Congress in 1921, continuing to organise campaigns towards *Swaraj* (self-rule). He was often seen with a *charkha*, a spinning wheel symbolising self-sufficiency.

Despite frequent imprisonment, Gandhi maintained peaceful resistance. A march to protest against a salt tax in 1930 – known as the '*Salt Satyagraha*', 'Satyagraha' meaning the insistence on truth – received worldwide news coverage. In 1942, Gandhi called for Britain to quit India, and the country finally gained independence in 1947. However, the country was split into Hindu-majority India and Muslim-majority Pakistan, a division that caused conflict. Gandhi was assassinated a year later by a man who believed he had favoured the Muslims of India, when in fact he had urged Hindus and Muslims to live together peacefully. The day after Gandhi's death, a million people gathered to pay their respects to the great soul who had worked all his life for their freedom.

ROSA LUXEMBURG

5 MARCH, 1871 – 15 JANUARY, 1919

> " Those who do not move,
> do not notice their chains. "

An uncompromising anti-war activist, the Polish-born German revolutionary ROSA LUXEMBURG worked passionately to promote freedom and fairness. Expressing her ideas in such works as *Reform or Revolution* (1899), she was interested in how society could best be structured to support the rights of all.

A vital force in the founding of the Polish Social Democratic Party and later the Spartacus League (which in time grew into the German Communist Party), she believed that capitalism was built on exploitation. Her view was that capitalism's need for constant economic growth – and therefore expansion into other countries – would create war, colonialism, gross inequality and the destruction of natural resources. For this she has been hailed by some as a real visionary for foreseeing the long-term impact of capitalism.

Luxemburg was a vocal opponent of the First World War. When it ended in 1918, Germany was left in turmoil as clashing political forces strove to take control. Luxemburg, along with fellow radical Karl Liebknecht, spearheaded the Spartacus League campaign to overthrow the government and create their concept of what a just and peaceful society could be. However, in Berlin in January 1919, she and Liebknecht were arrested by members of the Freikorps, private right-wing paramilitary groups. They were murdered, and Luxemburg's body was flung into Berlin's Landwehr Canal. Many members of the Freikorps went on to become part of the Nazi Party; if the Spartacus uprising had been successful, the twentieth century may have been very different.

HAROLD MOODY

8 OCTOBER, 1882 – 24 APRIL, 1947

" Our work ... has to be carried on to the hum of hostile planes and the boom of friendly guns. "

DR HAROLD MOODY was a ground-breaking ambassador for the rights of Black people in Britain in the 1900s. Jamaican-born into a devout Christian family, Moody came to England to study medicine in 1904. He soon encountered the racism that would motivate him to become an impassioned campaigner for racial equality. Although he qualified as top of his class at King's College London, he was refused work because of the colour of his skin; undeterred, Moody set up his own practice in Peckham, South East London. He was unafraid to marry a white woman – his colleague Olive Trantor, a nurse – at a time when mixed-race relationships were aggressively opposed. The couple went on to have six children.

Dr Moody was renowned for his compassion: before the advent of the National Health Service healthcare was expensive, but he treated poor children for free. Mindful of the discrimination and racial tension simmering in the UK after the First World War, Moody co-founded the League of Coloured Peoples to promote and protect the welfare of its members. The organisation aimed to champion the successes of Black people worldwide and campaign against prejudice. Moody fought for the educational, political, social and economic rights of Black people everywhere, and in 1943 was appointed to a government advisory committee on the welfare of non-Europeans.

Charismatic and principled in the face of racist hostility, Moody remained as the League's president until his death in 1947, having devoted his life to the fight for racial equality.

ELEANOR ROOSEVELT

11 OCTOBER, 1884 – 7 NOVEMBER, 1962

"
The future belongs to those who believe
in the beauty of their dreams.
"

A trail-blazing humanitarian, ELEANOR ROOSEVELT was born in New York into a family marked by both privilege and tragedy (a brother and both her parents died before she was ten years old). She came into the public eye as the wife of Franklin D Roosevelt, president of the United States from 1933 to 1945. However, she used her platform to develop her own influence as a human rights activist; she wrote newspaper and magazine columns, held press conferences and hosted a weekly radio show. This was unusual for a first lady and she caused controversy by advocating for child welfare, housing reform, racial equality and women's rights; later she also campaigned for the rights of Second World War refugees.

After her husband's death in 1945, Eleanor Roosevelt continued to be a political force. She urged the United States to join the United Nations, becoming its first delegate, and played a major role in drafting the Universal Declaration of Human Rights in 1948. In a world full of conflict and inequality, a declaration stating "All human beings are born free and equal in dignity and rights" was of huge and lasting significance. Being a driving force behind this extraordinary document, which speaks of 'the inherent dignity of all members of the human family', is her greatest legacy. In 1961 President John F Kennedy appointed Roosevelt the chair of the President's Commission on the Status of Women and she continued to be a great influence until her death a year later. Widely admired and respected, she was called 'First Lady of the World' by President Truman in recognition of her unwavering commitment to peace and equality.

NELSON MANDELA

18 JULY, 1918 – 5 DECEMBER, 2013

" If you want to make peace with your enemy, you have to work with your enemy. Then he becomes your partner. "

Born in Transkei, South Africa, NELSON MANDELA was the son of the chief of the Thembu tribe and became an inspirational global icon. He spearheaded the breakdown of apartheid (meaning 'apartness' – institutionalised racial segregation), and made history by becoming the first Black president of his country.

Mandela, who trained as a lawyer, joined an organisation called the African National Congress (ANC). Here, he joined in resistance against the ruling National Party's racist politics, which allowed the white population (less than ten per cent of the whole country) to oppress everyone else. This involvement led to him being charged with treason and Mandela was sentenced to life imprisonment. During his trial he made an extraordinary four-hour speech that ended with the words: "I have cherished the ideal of a democratic and free society in which all persons live together in harmony and with equal opportunities. It is an ideal which I hope to live for and to achieve. But if needs be, it is an ideal for which I am prepared to die."

During Mandela's 27-year imprisonment, his reputation as a powerful symbol of resistance grew; and, due to international pressure and for fear of a racial civil war, he was released by President F. W. de Klerk in 1990. Together Mandela and de Klerk negotiated the end of apartheid, which led to them both being awarded the Nobel Peace Prize in 1993. A year later Mandela was president. Deeply respected and much loved, he was known as 'Father of the Nation'.

KIM DAE-JUNG

6 JANUARY, 1924 – 18 AUGUST, 2009

"
Let's make history from now on.
"

Known as both 'the Nelson Mandela of Asia' and 'The Sunshine Politician', KIM DAE-JUNG was a politician who became president of South Korea, the first opposition candidate to achieve this. The trajectory of his career saw him come up against the dangerous dictatorial powers of the South Korean government; many attempts were made on his life as he campaigned ceaselessly for democracy.

Kim, a newspaper editor, became involved in politics when he witnessed ever-increasing levels of totalitarian oppression in South Korea. In 1969, President Park Chung Hee – who ruled the country as head of a military dictatorship – sought to force through legal changes so he could rule for a third term. Kim gave an impassioned speech opposing the scheme; his bravery led to him being chosen as the presidential candidate for the New Democratic Party in 1971, and he helped to inspire widespread pro-democracy demonstrations across South Korea. So threatening was his voice to the government that there followed years of turbulence for Kim, as he endured assassination attempts and periods of exile and imprisonment. After decades of commitment he became president in 1998.

As president, Kim's 'Sunshine Policy' sought a peaceful reunification between North and South Korea, which had been at war since 1950. In 2000, Kim arranged a summit meeting with North Korea's leader Kim Jong-il and, in doing so, allowed family members who had been separated for over forty years to meet again. Kim and Kim Jong-il signed a joint declaration paving the way for mutual respect and trust and an easing of military tensions. It was this Sunshine Policy and his lifelong commitment to democracy which led to Kim being awarded the Nobel Peace Prize in 2000.

MARTIN LUTHER KING, JR.

15 JANUARY, 1929 – 4 APRIL 1968

" Darkness cannot drive out darkness;
only light can do that. "

A Baptist minister who became the most prominent and beloved voice of the American civil rights movement, Martin Luther King, Jr. promoted peaceful methods of dissent in the face of the racist violence that eventually killed him.

An exceptional student, King went on to become a minister, basing his non-violent methods of civil disobedience on the teachings of Christ and the activism of Gandhi. He led many significant civil rights actions, such as the year-long Montgomery Bus Boycott, sparked by the arrest of Rosa Parks, who had refused to give up her bus seat to a white man and was thrown in jail. During the protest, King's house was bombed and he was arrested and jailed, but eventually the United States District Court prohibited racial segregation on all Montgomery public buses.

In his *I Have a Dream* speech, given to more than a quarter of a million people during the civil rights march on Washington in 1963, King spoke about a world where people "... will not be judged by the colour of their skin but by the content of their character". The march demanded the end of racial discrimination in employment and of racial segregation in schools. A year later King was awarded the Nobel Peace Prize for his commitment to achieving racial equality through non-violent means.

King's recognition meant he was both celebrated and under constant threat. The day after giving his *I've Been to the Mountaintop* speech in Memphis in April 1968, he was shot and killed in an act of racist violence. King's shining legacy, however, lives on, and he continues to inspire generations of those who strive for equality for all.

SHIRIN EBADI

21 JUNE, 1947 –

I maintain that nothing useful and lasting can emerge from violence.

Born in Hamadan in Iran, Shirin Ebadi is a human rights activist, lawyer, former judge and writer. She was awarded the Nobel Peace Prize in 2003 for her commitment to human rights and democracy, particularly in relation to women and children.

An outstanding student, Ebadi earned her law degree, qualified as a judge and became head of the city court of Tehran, the capital city of Iran. However in 1979, the Islamic Revolution – in part a conservative backlash against Iran being affected by Western influences – deprived women of human rights. Demoted to a clerk in the very court she had presided over, Ebadi resigned in protest and struggled for years to obtain a license to practise law again.

During this time she wrote many books and articles. In 1992 she regained her license and devoted her energies to defending people. She helped draft a law against the physical abuse of children and campaigned for women to have the right to divorce their husbands. In 2001, Ebadi helped found the Defenders of Human Rights Center in Tehran. She enraged government officials by distributing evidence implicating them in the murders of university students in 1999, and was jailed for three weeks.

Her courageous work led to her being honoured internationally but also endangered her life at home. In 2008 the Defenders of Human Rights Center was closed by the government and the following year Ebadi's Nobel Prize medal was confiscated by the Iranian authorities. Ebadi left Iran, never to return. Based in the UK, this extraordinary activist for peace and freedom continues to raise her voice about the need for reforms in Iran.

MO MOWLAM

18 SEPTEMBER, 1949 – 19 AUGUST, 2005

" *It takes courage to push things forward.* "

British rule in Ireland has sparked conflict and resistance since the twelfth century. In 1916, the Easter Rising in Dublin led to civil war. This resulted in the division of the island into the Republic of Ireland (a newly formed, independent state) and Northern Ireland (which remained a part of the United Kingdom). Within Northern Ireland conflicts raged between the Republicans who wanted Northern Ireland to be a part of the independent state, and the Loyalists, who defended things as they were. The violence intensified in the 1960s to include the police, and British troops were sent in.

As Shadow Secretary of State for Northern Ireland in 1994, and then Secretary of State for Northern Ireland in 1997, the English Labour politician MO MOWLAM was a driving force towards achieving peace in Northern Ireland. A courageous communicator, her outspoken openness, charm and humanity made an impact on the rival groups involved in what was known as 'The Troubles'. She helped break down barriers between the warring factors and participated in discussions that eventually evolved into the Good Friday Agreement, which was reached on April 10th, 1998. This historic agreement resulted in a new government being formed that would allow for power to be shared between both sides.

Mowlam was a hugely popular figure in British politics, and her early death due to cancer at the age of 55 was met with great sadness. She will be remembered for her dynamism, straightforwardness and humour, in addition to the enormous contribution she made towards peace in Northern Ireland.

RIGOBERTA MENCHÚ

9 JANUARY, 1959 –

"
When you are convinced your cause is just,
you fight for it.
"

A human rights activist and feminist who was awarded the Nobel Peace Prize in 1992, RIGOBERTA MENCHÚ has devoted her life to giving voice to the plight of indigenous people, in her home country of Guatemala and around the world.

As the child of an impoverished indigenous family of Mayan K'iche' descent, Menchú experienced injustice within a changing society. In 1960, a brutal civil war began in Guatemala against the Mayan people, initiated by the military dictatorship and wealthy landowners. Countless Mayans were murdered and displaced. Menchú and her family travelled peacefully amongst rural communities, teaching indigenous people their rights and encouraging them to denounce the violent crimes of the government. Their courage as activists made them vulnerable to harm. Menchú fled to exile in Mexico after her mother, father and brother were murdered.

In Mexico, Menchú co-founded the United Republic of Guatemalan Opposition and became a powerful public speaker, putting pressure on the Guatemalan government to stop their violent campaigns against indigenous people. In 1982, the publication of her book *My Name is Rigoberta Menchú* gained her prominence on the world stage. This led to her being awarded the Nobel Peace Prize; she used the prize money to found the Rigoberta Menchú Tum Foundation, which provides healthcare and advocacy to Guatemalan Indians and seeks to build unity between indigenous groups. Her striving to negotiate an end to the conflict helped pave a path to the peace agreement that was signed in 1996, bringing the civil war to an end. Menchú became an ambassador for the world's indigenous peoples and continues to work for peace today.

LEYMAH GBOWEE

1 FEBRUARY, 1972 –

 I'm a serious optimist. "

Born in Liberia, the indomitable LEYMAH GBOWEE led a multitude of women to demand peace in her war-torn country – and achieve it.

Gbowee was one of the millions of people affected by years of bloodshed during the two Liberian Civil Wars (1989–1997 and 1999–2003). She fled to Ghana, but near-starvation forced her to return with her young family to Liberia. In response to the chaos around her, she volunteered with the Trauma Healing and Reconciliation Program. This was the first step towards her becoming a world-renowned peace activist, and joint winner of the Nobel Peace Prize in 2011.

Working to rehabilitate ex-child soldiers brutalised by war, Gbowee then joined the Women in Peacebuilding Network (WIPNET), teaching women about conflict resolution. As more and more women were inspired to protest peacefully against the war that blighted their lives, a new group was formed: Women of Liberia Mass Action for Peace. All dressed in white, and a mixture of all classes and religions, this huge group of women picketed government buildings and demanded an end to the abuses of war.

Gbowee put pressure on Liberia's president, Charles Taylor, to attend peace talks with the rebel groups involved in the conflict – during which she and hundreds of women surrounded the building and refused to let anyone leave until an agreement was reached. Their actions changed history and ended 14 years of war. Gbowee has been recognised with numerous awards for her fearless commitment to peace and the empowerment of women.

JOËL GUSTAVE NANA NGONGANG

5 FEBRUARY, 1982 – 15 OCTOBER, 2015

 Only Africans can speak for Africans.

JOËL GUSTAVE NANA NGONGANG was a shining light for LGBT rights in Africa: the boundless energy of his commitment supported the freedoms and rights of many to live peaceful lives.

Born in Cameroon, Ngongang trained as a lawyer – he specialised in International Human Rights Law – and could speak six languages. A big part of his focus as an LGBT rights activist was supporting awareness of HIV throughout Africa, particularly in relation to gay and bisexual men. He was a Pan Africanist – he believed in the political unity of all African people, wherever they lived – and he spoke passionately about the importance of African voices not being drowned out by Western organisations: "As LGBT Africans, we feel the vestiges of the long European colonial presence in our continent."

In order to fight prejudice against LGBT people in Africa, Ngongang became deeply involved in organisations at local, national and international levels. In 2005, the case of the Yaoundé Eleven brought his powerful advocacy for LGBT causes to global attention. Eleven men were arrested and imprisoned on 'suspicion of homosexuality' and Ngongang dedicated himself to publicising this injustice. He wrote and spoke widely about the issues involved and was a frequent media commentator. His efforts contributed greatly to the United Nations Working Group on Arbitrary Detention declaring their incarceration contrary to the International Covenant on Civil and Political Rights, and the Yaoundé Eleven were freed.

Ngongang died in 2015 after an illness; his unstinting, forceful activism for the LGBT community in Africa and beyond had enormous impact, and is his legacy.

MALALA YOUSAFZAI

12 JULY, 1997 –

 When the whole world is silent,
even one voice becomes powerful.

MALALA YOUSAFZAI is a courageous advocate for female education and human rights, campaigning for every child to have access to an education. She survived an attempt on her life at the age of 15 and went on to be the youngest person ever to receive the Nobel Peace Prize – awarded to her in 2014 when she was 17 years old.

Malala was born in 1997 in Mingora, Pakistan. Many communities in Pakistan did not allow girls an education, but Malala was able to attend a school for girls run by her father. But by the time she was 10, a strict fundamentalist Muslim sect – called the Taliban – began to take over the district she lived in, demanding that anyone female be denied human rights, such as an education and the right to vote.

In defiance of this, and encouraged by her father, Malala wrote a blog, *Diary of a Pakistani Schoolgirl*, exposing how the Taliban were suppressing the education and rights of girls in the region. Enraged, the Taliban sent a gunman to kill Malala on her way home from school, and she was shot. Fighting for her life, she was flown to England where she not only recovered, but went on to speak all over the world about the importance of education for all children. A true hero, her message is one of peace, saying of the man who shot her: "Even if there is a gun in my hand and he stands in front of me. I would not shoot him. ... This is what my soul is telling me, be peaceful and love everyone."

X GONZÁLEZ

11 NOVEMBER, 1999 –

" We call B.S. "

On 14 February, 2018, X González (born Emma Wise González) was attending a class at the Marjory Stoneman Douglas High School in Parkland, Florida, USA. An ordinary day turned into one of terror as a shooter opened fire on students and staff, killing 17 people and wounding more. González and their classmates took cover as SWAT teams swarmed through the school to apprehend the killer.

Fuelled by grief and outrage, González channelled their pain into a searing speech demanding the tightening of gun control laws. At a rally just three days after the massacre, in response to the claims of President Trump and others that tougher gun laws wouldn't decrease gun violence, González stated, "We call B.S." – maintaining that such a stance was blatantly untrue.

Their speech went viral, and González used this new high profile to reinforce the message that gun control in America needed a complete overhaul. They and other Parkland survivors organised the nationwide March for Our Lives on 24 March 24, 2018. In a remarkable piece of activism, González gave a speech during the protest naming all the murdered victims of the Parkland massacre and then fell silent, as the world watched. Their speech and the silence that followed lasted the same amount of time as it had taken the killer to gun down all those people: six minutes and thirty seconds.

Inspired by the protest, the Florida Legislature passed the Marjory Stoneman Douglas High School Public Safety Act, which introduced significant restrictions on acquiring firearms. The governor said to the students of the school, "You made your voices heard ... you fought until there was change". At the forefront of that change stood X González, and they continue their work in peace activism today.

Glossary

ACTIVISM – the practice of taking direct and continued action to achieve social or political change

AMBASSADOR – a diplomatic official sent by one sovereign or state to reside in another as its representative; also, an unofficial or official representative of a movement or ideal

APARTHEID – meaning 'apartness' in the language of Afrikaans in South Africa: a system or policy that segregates people on the basis of their race

ASSIMILATION – a process of taking in, making similar; historically where groups and individuals of different heritages acquire the habits and attitudes of the dominant societal culture

CAPITALISM – an economic and political system in which property, trade and industry are owned and controlled by private individuals in order to make a profit

COLONIALISM – when one country takes full or partial control of another, occupies it with settlers and maintains cultural, social, political and economic domination over the indigenous peoples

COMPASSION – the feeling of being deeply moved by another's suffering, and motivated to ease it

DEMOCRACY – a system where the greatest number of votes cast by its members in an election determines who governs it

DICTATORSHIP – governmental rule by a dictator: where one person or an exclusive group has total power over the state, limiting the rights of its citizens and obliterating freedom of speech

DISSENT – to hold opinions in opposition to those officially held; to withhold approval

ETHICS – a personal sense of what is right and wrong, which determines how an individual behaves; also, the branch of knowledge that deals with these moral principles

EMPOWERMENT – the giving of power to someone; the process of becoming more powerful; to have control over one's own rights and life

HUMANITARIAN – someone who seeks to support human welfare through saving lives, reducing suffering and increasing the opportunity for peace and happiness

INCARCERATION – the state of imprisonment; being confined within a prison or jail

INDIGENOUS – someone or something who originates or occurs naturally in a particular place; native

LGBT – initials that stand for Lesbian, Gay, Bisexual and Transgender

LEGACY – something – physical, monetary or conceptual – passed from one person or generation to another after their death

NEGOTIATE – to bargain or discuss an issue with the objective of gaining an agreement that suits both sides in an argument or conflict

NOBEL PEACE PRIZE – one of the five Nobel Prizes set up by the Swedish inventor, engineer and businessman Alfred Nobel; awarded annually since March 1901 to an individual or individuals who have done the most to promote peace in the world

OPPRESSION – that which restricts the freedom and happiness of others or another via an unjust use of power

PACIFISM – the opposition to war, violence and militarism; the belief that disputes should be settled peacefully

PRINCIPLED – the quality of acting with honesty and integrity, in accordance with perceived moral values of right and wrong

PROFOUND – intense, impactful, meaningful

RESISTANCE – the refusal to obey, comply with or accept something

SEGREGATION – the setting apart or separation of one kind of person or thing from another, or from the main group

SWAT TEAMS – law enforcement units with specialised weapons; SWAT stands for: special weapons and tactics

TAOISM – a philosophical tradition of Chinese origin based on the writings of Laozi, that advocates living in harmony with the Tao, which means 'the way' and is described as the source of existence. This harmony can be achieved via the 'Three Treasures': compassion, frugality and humility

TOTALITARIAN – a system of government which demands absolute control over all aspects of individual life

TURBULENCE – the state of being turbulent – agitated, violent, unsteady

UNCOMPROMISING – an unwillingness to bend to another's will; to refuse to make concessions to others or change one's opinions

UNITY – the state of oneness; of being united, joined into a whole; being in alignment

VIRTUE – excellent moral standards shown by behaviour

Index